T0171624

Also by Nancy Ferrin:

Where is My Baby? . . .
A Mother's Message of Hope and Healing,
Winepress Publishing, 2006.

WHEN A PRODIGAL BREAKS YOUR HEART

THE SEARCH FOR UNDERSTANDING AND HOPE

NANCY FERRIN

WESTBOW
PRESS
A DIVISION OF THOMAS NELSON

WestBow Press books may be ordered through booksellers or by contacting:

WestBow Press
A Division of Thomas Nelson
1663 Liberty Drive
Bloomington, IN 47403
www.westbowpress.com
1-(866) 928-1240

ISBN: 978-1-4497-6508-8 (sc)
ISBN: 978-1-4497-6507-1 (e)
ISBN: 978-1-4497-6559-0 (hc)

Library of Congress Control Number: 2012915763

Printed in the United States of America

WestBow Press rev. date: 09/26/2012

TABLE OF CONTENTS

Introduction ix

Chapter 1:   Denial   1
             Basic Question: What is really going on?
             Heart string: This is no surprise to God.

Chapter 2:   Fear   9
             Basic question: Where will this lead?
             Heart string: God is still in control and His
             peace is available.

Chapter 3:   Confusion   19
             Basic question: What should be done? Where do
             I begin?
             Heart string: God is not the Author of
             confusion; He has a plan.

Chapter 4:   Guilt   29
             Basic question: What did I do wrong? Why
             wasn't I a better parent?
             Heart string: Satan is the accuser; God
             understands, forgives and restores.

Chapter 5:   Sorrow   37
             Basic question: How did it get to this point?
             Heart string: God is with me and He will wipe
             away my tears.

Chapter 6:   Shame   45
              Basic question: What will others think? How can
                 I face my friends?
              Heart string: Seek to please God and not other
                 people.

Chapter 7:   Frustration   55
              Basic question: What can I do to stop this?
              Heart string: Apart from Him I can do
                 absolutely nothing. My job is to abide in
                 Christ.

Chapter 8:   Anger   63
              Basic question: How could he do this to me and
                 to himself?
              Heart string: God wants me to forgive and
                 stands ready to diffuse the entire situation.

Chapter 9:   Release   73
              Basic question: Where can I put my trust and
                 find rest?
              Heart string: God is good and wise and loving
                 toward all He has made; He is worthy of my
                 complete trust; He is watching over my child
                 in love.

Chapter 10:   Hope   87
              Basic question: When will my prodigal come
                 home?
              Heart string: God can do all things; nothing is
                 impossible for Him.

Reflections   Closing thoughts from each prodigal, and
              personal encouragement to the reader   97

This book is dedicated to my precious children, David and his wife, Emily, Jonathan, Daniel, Mindy, and Christopher. You are dearly loved and add such joy and purpose to my life. We have learned a lot together on this journey of life and I am honored to be your mother. May the Lord guide and bless you each step of the way. You make me proud. xxoo

INTRODUCTION

"Where did I go wrong?" is the question burning in the hearts of many discouraged parents. With every passing year, I meet people who are confused, ashamed, and worried about the dangerous choices their teens and adult children continue to make. Each generation faces challenges and temptation. Yet the downward spiral seems to be moving with increased speed and destruction. The Bible warns this pattern will continue and worsen until the Lord's return. So it is imperative we find hope and strength from others who have traveled this path.

My mother's heart has been broken repeatedly because of the choices of my beloved prodigals. A "prodigal" is one who chooses a wasteful and/or reckless lifestyle. Despite being raised with godly standards and the truth of God's Word, they turn away for a season (or longer) and it can be especially perplexing. This book explores ten emotions common among parents of prodigals. Each chapter provides a "heart string" to help us re-focus and remember truth in the midst of the pain. My heart's desire is that you will be encouraged by what is shared and will join me in proclaiming with full confidence, "The Lord is faithful in all things and I will continue to trust Him."

Please take advantage of the questions at the end of each chapter to help with processing your unique situation. May the Lord provide insight and strength for each reader and freedom for each beloved prodigal, according to His timing and His sovereign will.

CHAPTER ONE

DENIAL

Basic Question: What is really going on?
Heart string: This is no surprise to God.

The realization comes slowly, doesn't it? "He's just a difficult child". "The pressures of school are really getting to him". "If only she would find better friends." "I need to spend more time with her and then she'll be more cooperative." Thoughts like these occupied my mind when troubles began with each child. I wanted an easy fix. I desperately attempted to justify and rationalize the unacceptable actions and attitudes that were surfacing. This was not the plan!

Danny, our third son, was always such a joy to be around. His sense of humor, his love for life, and his smile were all endearing qualities to a mother's heart. Early school years went without incident. He made good grades and had lots of friends. Danny enjoyed sports and was outgoing and cooperative. When things began to turn around at school, I was surprised and unprepared. He attended a small Christian school and by eighth grade he was in danger of being asked to leave. I decided the environment was too "restrictive" and the administrators and teachers just didn't appreciate Danny's delightful personality. He was not a serious student like his older brothers and maybe he just didn't fit the mold. We transferred him to public school. About a year later, Danny wanted to return to the small, Christian school. He was a bit overwhelmed by the size of the public school and he missed his friends. We obliged, but it didn't last long. Things continued to escalate. His grades were so bad that he couldn't participate in JV sports. That was the beginning of the end, in my opinion. Danny was a great basketball and baseball player, but without that outlet, he began a downward spiral. Soon he was back to public school, and then came the moment I never dreamed would happen. Upon turning eighteen, Danny quit school. I was heartbroken but it was just the beginning of his prodigal journey.

We all have basic expectations for our kids. Surely if we raise them with godly, moral values, they will embrace them and follow the straight and narrow path. If we provide a comfortable and safe home, they will respond with gratitude and appreciation for all they have, right? Well, not always. How about this widely believed thought? Since my child has been encased in years of prayer, he will be delivered from temptation and guided on paths of righteousness. It seems foolproof. Do it "right" and they will turn out "right"; case closed. So when things begin to happen to the contrary, it takes awhile to recognize what is really going on.

When my children were young and still pretty much "under control", I was so naïve about what was ahead. Whenever I witnessed someone else's rebellious child, I clung to the belief *my* child would never behave like that! The innocence of childhood, the optimism of young parents, and our own prideful thoughts insulate us from the "dark side" for a time. When my son, and later my daughter, started to exhibit questionable behavior patterns, I was totally unprepared. We can be clueless for a time . . . but not forever.

Gradually it dawned on me Danny's bad days were far outnumbering the good ones. I struggled with disbelief and asked myself, "What is going on with my son? Could it be he is choosing the path of rebellion? Nonsense! That could never be!" Like most parents, my initial conclusion was his problems were due to someone else—other authorities in his life such as the teachers, the school principal, the basketball coach. "They just don't understand him. In fact, I bet they don't even like him. They are way too hard on him." *Denial. Rationalization. Lies that seem so believable.*

When that no longer placates us we switch to blaming peers. "Those kids are no good! They are leading her down a slippery slope. If I could just get her away from that crowd things would be different." Next we start to blame ourselves and our family. "No wonder he is acting out, our home is in chaos." "If only my husband would be a better role model and spend more time with him . . ." "If only I wasn't so busy all the time. Poor child. We are really messing him up." *Denial. Rationalization. Lies that seem so believable.* So many of us blame ourselves.

> Mindy has always adored her older brother, Danny. As the only daughter in the family, she was treated like a princess in those early years, especially by her daddy. She could get her way by flashing those beautiful brown eyes. She had some struggles in school, but was primarily a quiet, shy little girl in public. Behind the scenes she was rather strong willed and moody. I began to recognize academic delays in the fifth grade, but nothing was diagnosed as a "real problem". Early teen years brought stress and lots of drama as she succumbed to peer pressure. But I was slow to recognize that Mindy was choosing a path similar to Danny.

Denial is a protective layer for our hearts. It keeps us away from the painful truth but it only lasts for a while. Eventually it becomes clear the problem is not primarily with the school, or the peer group, or even our imperfect homes. The problem is a child who is bent on rebellion. It can take us by surprise, but it is no surprise to

God. He weeps with us and He cares about our broken hearts and shattered expectations. He knew this would happen and despite the fallout, we must remember He is still in control.

Once we recognize there is a serious problem, we tend to experience other types of denial such as being unable to recognize the truth about the path our child has chosen, the seriousness of the potential consequences, and the impact on other family members. Having a sympathetic ear may mean we easily buy into the child's defective reasoning and begin to believe the excuses and lies. I had a hard time accepting my prodigals were not always truthful. They could be so convincing and I wanted so much to believe them. *Denial. Rationalization. Lies that seem so believable.* We must have the courage to see beyond the lies.

We may be in denial concerning the type and extent of help needed. I remember sitting for hours in the emergency room waiting for a psychological consult for my daughter. We had been there just the night before for hours and I was weary. If I'd had my way, I'd have taken her home to just "start over". But since she was in the juvenile probation system, our probation officer saw the situation much more clearly. She persisted and Mindy ended up in psychiatric care for a brief time. My denial might have prevented her from getting the extent of help needed at that time.

Once things begin to improve in the life of our prodigal, it is such an emotional relief. Yet often the path has more unexpected twists and complacency is not our best choice. Beware of the denial that refuses to acknowledge the return of destructive patterns. Once again, denial sneaks in as a protective layer for our hearts. But it is important to remain alert and discerning.

The prodigal's recovery is bound to be a long process. Those who reject their faith for a season and knowingly turn from God are especially vulnerable. Because God loves them, He pursues them and the enemy eagerly engages in the battle. The struggles and temptations are magnified because of the witness of God's Holy Spirit resulting in turmoil within. Denial may be a protection for our hearts, but in order to help our prodigals we need courage to see the truth.

FOR PERSONAL REFLECTION

1. How have you been tempted to justify the behavior of your prodigal?

2. What incident brought the truth to light for you?

3. Briefly describe the dangers related to your prodigal's current path.

Pray: Ask the Lord to reveal what you need to know about the seriousness of your situation and for the courage to see the truth, no matter how painful.

CHAPTER TWO

FEAR

Basic question: Where will this lead?
Heart string: God is still in control and His
peace is available.

God's Word describes two types of fear. One is a healthy, reverential fear of God – a respect for His power and an awe of His perfection. We are told the "fear of God is the beginning of wisdom" (Psalm 111:20). It is appropriate to fear the Almighty. It is also appropriate to fear impending danger. We all teach our children to be careful when crossing the street because of the danger of oncoming traffic. We teach them to respect boundaries placed for their safety. When my three oldest boys were young I recall a visit to the top of a mountain by tramway. Once at the top their father insisted on taking them "exploring" but my fear kept me safely inside the snack shop at the summit. Years later he told me about a few "close calls" and I was reminded of those fearful moments – realizing that the fear was somewhat justified!

By contrast, many times in Scripture we are told to "fear not". There are times when our fear is unfounded and inappropriate.

Fear can become a destructive preoccupation with what *might* be ahead – not based on facts, but on feelings. The fear of the unknown, the fear of death, the fear of receiving bad news are all examples of times when it is best to trust and not fear. God is in control.

> Not long ago I experienced a fear I had never known before. At that time Mindy was court assigned to a nearby girls' home. It was her first long-term placement and, in retrospect, it was quite nice. She had a private room in a beautiful old home and they were graciously escorting her by van to her hometown high school. But one morning, after disembarking at the school, she abruptly left campus. When she didn't return for the ride home, the school, the police, and the girls' home all alerted me. As you can imagine, fear grew in me during the weeks she was missing. I didn't know where she was, who she was with, or what she was doing. There seemed to be endless news reports about kidnappings, rapists and murders. It was torture. Fear was crouching behind every door.
>
> If I had chosen to turn away from God at that time, I would have been destroyed. But instead, I clung to God's promises and was refreshed as His peace flooded my heart and mind. I was able

to function, to think calmly, to sleep at night, to enjoy the beauty of the flowering trees and beautiful skies, and to make time for visits with concerned friends. It was a time of reflection and sadness, but knowing God was in control made all the difference.

Fear has been described using the acronym, "False Evidence Appearing Real". Fears are often unfounded, exaggerated ideas that seem believable and possible. We need to beware of the tendency of our mind to carry us far away from reality. However, fear is not always an exaggeration. It is right to acknowledge the dangers that exist when our prodigal chooses an unsafe path. In every situation we must be quick to anchor our heart and mind to this truth: God has not left His governing position. He is *always* in control and we can trust Him.

The worst fear I experienced during my seasons of parenting prodigals came when my daughter was involved with drugs. In a moment, she could become extremely angry and disruptive. Her language was coarse and vulgar. The slightest provocation made her defensive and confrontational. I hardly recognized her as the former "princess" of the house. Because of her propensity to steal things, we installed locks on all the bedroom doors. Can you imagine locking your room in your own home in order to protect your valuables from a family member? It was inconceivable and I resisted. But one night uncontrollable fear rose up in my heart. The peace I had clung to was replaced by a sense of impending doom. I was afraid of my daughter and I locked myself in my room.

Suddenly I remembered there was a second, unlocked door in my room leading to a small bedroom. I raced to slide the sewing machine over to block the door from opening. When it was almost in place, someone began to push that door in – I screamed and cried and lost control. It was a nightmare and I felt like I was coming unglued. My son came to the rescue and took over the situation. I will never forget that night. Mindy was only weeks away from turning 18 so I was still legally required to provide a home for her. In her fury that night, she wanted to leave and we all knew it was the best option. I can still hear Danny's words to her (one former prodigal to another), "Go ahead and leave, but this time we won't be calling the police to find you, we'll be locking the doors behind you." She did and we did.

Some may think this action was too harsh. Please trust me. The story is far more complicated. In retrospect, it was the right action and seems to have prevented future outbursts. She left behind the role of the violent, raging rebel and turned her back on drugs, for a season (praise God!). Peace and sanity returned to our home and Mindy chose to live elsewhere. I enjoyed my time with her whenever she made contact and she was, once again, a delight. In this case, the boundary worked and fear was stopped in its track.

When things seem most out of control, God is still in control. He remains the Solid Rock and the only One who understands *every detail* of our complicated situations. His Word tells us clearly to turn to Him whenever we are filled with anxiety and fear. Early in Danny's prodigal years there was a time when God used a familiar bible promise to get my attention in an unforgettable way.

> I awoke at three a.m. and realized Danny wasn't home. I remember the blue chair in the living room where I sat – funny how some memories are like photographs. As I sat and waited for his return I cried and prayed. My thoughts were invaded by arrows from the enemy. "There isn't anything you can do. You have no idea where he is or what he is doing. Your prayers can't bring him home. You are a fool. Just go to bed and hope he makes it home. Sitting here and praying does nothing to change things." Immediately the Spirit nudged me to recite aloud Philippians 4:6-7. I resisted initially, agreeing with the inner voice that nothing would change. But then, almost arrogantly, I resigned

my will to the Spirit's prompting and started to say it aloud.

My paraphrase went something like this: "Do not be anxious about anything". I was almost spitting out those words. I was angry with the accusing voice in my head, angry with the situation, angry with my prodigal. I continued, "But in everything, with prayer and petition with thanksgiving". With *thanksgiving*? How can I be thankful at a moment like this? But a softening was taking place in my heart. Once more I continued, "Let your requests be made known to God." Oh Lord, You know my request. Please, please bring my son home! "And the peace of God," Yes, His peace was really moving in! "Which passes all understanding, will guard your heart and your mind in Christ Jesus." It was almost like a script for a movie because just as I finished reciting the verse, car headlights appeared in the driveway and my boy was home.

Do you have fear related to your prodigal? Perhaps you fear for his safety. Perhaps you fear for your safety. God is in control. He really is. God knows the details of your situation and He already knows the outcome. Don't listen to the voice of the accuser. Turn to God in prayer. Let Him remind you of truths like these found in His Word:

"Fear not, for I am with you; be not dismayed, for I am your God. I will strengthen you, yes, I will help you. I will uphold you with My righteous right hand." (Isaiah 41:1)

"The Lord is my light and my salvation; whom shall I fear? The Lord is the strength of my life; of whom shall I be afraid?" (Psalm 27:1)

Speaking of the one who trusts in God, "He will have no fear of bad news, his heart is steadfast, trusting in the Lord. His heart is secure, he will have no fear." (Psalm 112:7-8a)

"For God did not give us a spirit of timidity (fear), but a spirit of power, of love and of self discipline." (2 Timothy 1:7)

That night in the chair was a powerful turning point. Only on rare occasions since then have I sat up to wait and worry when one of my prodigals is late coming home. God never repeated that striking demonstration of His power, but it is etched upon my heart. Remember God is never obligated to respond to our prayers in dramatic ways, yet sometimes He does. Don't miss the lessons He sends. Some may be amazing, but usually the peace comes as we listen to His still small voice. God wants to heal your fearful heart. Recognize His voice as He speaks once more, "Trust Me, I AM in control".

FOR PERSONAL REFLECTION

1. Have you been given a life-impacting reminder of God's power? Describe.

2. What fears are you holding that need to be released? What fear is the most overwhelming?

3. Choose a helpful bible verse and describe how it applies to your life.

Pray: Put Philippians 4:6-7 into practice as you release your worries and fears to God and receive His indescribable peace as a divine covering for your heart and mind. The Message translation for those verses is so beautiful. "Don't fret or worry. Instead of worrying, pray. Let petitions and praises shape your worries into prayers, letting God know your concerns. Before you know it, a sense of God's wholeness, everything coming together for good, will come and *settle you down*. It's wonderful what happens when Christ displaces worry at the center of your life."

CHAPTER THREE

CONFUSION

Basic question: What should be done? Where do I begin?
Heart string: God is not the Author of confusion;
He has a plan.

When my children were young, the house was often filled with lots of activity and confusion. On a typical school morning, I remember making a line of sandwiches and attaching small sticky notes on each baggie to identify its owner. Often there was a flurry of activity just before the bus was due to arrive. "Where is my blue notebook?" "Who moved my shoes?" "Mom, you need to sign these papers for my English teacher!" I tried to have everything organized, but I didn't have the finesse of Martha Stewart. Somehow we made it through those busy years.

As the older boys entered their teen years, I became somewhat confused about all the changes taking place. I felt strangely saddened by their growing independent spirit and longed for the days when they wanted to hold my hand or sit on my lap. My advice wasn't considered as valuable as it had been a few years earlier. I recognized conflicting emotions within them, too, as they dealt with the onset of adolescence. These confusing times were normal and mixed with moments of unbounded joy as I saw them growing and maturing before my eyes.

But the confusion that comes from the heartbreak of rebellion is much more serious. It can become a paralyzing force as we desperately try to find the best path. People try to help with heartfelt advice, stories they think will help, and warnings we have already considered a million times. Our thoughts can race in a futile attempt to solve the problem.

> When Danny disclosed to me he was trapped by serious drug use, I tried very hard to remain calm and reassuring. I wanted him to have hope and to see my love for him was unconditional. As soon as I was alone, I poured over internet pages, trying to find the best solution. The search was unending and confusing. There are so many treatment centers—in-patient options, out-patient therapy groups, experts advocating parental support, and others saying to kick them out so they would hit "rock bottom". I was confused about what to do, about how bad the situation was, and about how it had all happened right under my nose! Thoughts raced and my insecurities grew. How could I make a decision? The confusion was suffocating.

Dr. James Dobson in his book, *When God Doesn't Make Sense*, gives this warning. "It is an incorrect view of Scripture to say that we will always comprehend what God is doing and how our suffering and disappointments fit into His plan. Sooner or later, most of us will come to a point where it appears that God has lost control – or interest – in the affairs of people. It is only an illusion, but one with dangerous implications for spiritual and mental health. Interestingly enough, pain and suffering do not cause the greatest damage. *Confusion* is the factor that shreds one's faith."

When confusion stirs in our heart, the best thing to do is take a deep breath and *stop*—stop trying to take full responsibility, stop trying to figure out why it happened, stop trying to fix it, and stop trying to find the "one-and-only ideal solution". The journey with our prodigal can take years, and the degree of confusion will vary from month to month. Some steps we choose will prove helpful; others might take us backwards. I am reminded once again to cling to the truth that God is in control and He has a plan. Many times His plan seems illusive, but God's word instructs us to wait patiently for His leading, to listen for His still, small voice, and to trust in His unfailing love.

> Confusion exploded in my heart and mind as I waited for the court's decision regarding placement for my daughter. Which option is the best? Where will she receive the help she needs? What location will be the most therapeutic? Where are the

people who will have a strong, positive impact on her young life? I was unsure about the options available, forced to rely on the judgment of the "experts", and burdened by the severity of this decision. Once again, I had to stop the endless analysis and trust God to carry out His best plan for Mindy.

More confusion entered when the first place she was sent didn't work out since she ran away. Months later, the second place didn't work out for the same reason. To my dismay, the court sent her home and denied the treatment program I thought surely was God's plan. Mindy spent nearly two years in the juvenile probation system, incurred an enormous debt that we must pay back to the state, and was not significantly helped. It seems like wasted time, wasted money and wasted pain. I lost valuable time with my teenage daughter. Where was God's plan? Had we missed it?

There are times when it is possible to look back and recognize the wisdom of God's unfolding plan. When I was in college, I wanted to be a high school math teacher. I had no interest in computers, but the math major requirement included lots of computer science courses. For over twenty years I was able to work part-time from home as a computer programmer. While the teaching skills were a blessing for bible studies and retreat speaking, God knew what job would best supplement our family's income. Decades later, the programming job came to an abrupt end and now I am recertified, working as a high school math teacher. I marvel at the outworking of His plan for my employment.

Yet at other times, the twisting of our path makes no sense. In the midst of the pain and confusion of the moment, we need to cling to the strong belief that God always has a plan. His plan, we are told in Scripture, is for our good and His glory. By faith we must believe God will ultimately be glorified by the stories of our dear prodigals.

Often I wish I could undo the decisions that were made by the court regarding Mindy. Yet the judge gave her so many chances to choose the right path. Mindy could have followed the guidelines of probation and it would have been over in just a few months. She could have cooperated and avoided placement. Once in placement, she could have stayed and not run away! Surely there were many people trying to cheer her on in the right direction. Many friends were praying along with me for God's will in each decision. But looking back at the months of "treatment" with no apparent benefit is confusing and disconcerting. Could it have been handled differently? Did the court system only make things more complicated and worse?

Much of the confusion we experience is related to the age-old struggle between the interworking of God's will and our free will. God is not the Author of confusion, but we are so prone to veer off the best path. Comfort comes in recognizing God as the great Redeemer. Despite our wrong choices and mistakes, He can make our path straight. He can use the pain and difficulties to teach us and to shape us into the image of His Son. In God's economy, pain is a prerequisite for transformation.

Over and over again God births good results from painful experiences. His plan is often hidden until years later. After serving as a women's ministry director for a number of years, I sensed God leading me to leave the church. The situation was complicated and it was hard to leave such precious friends. But years later, I rejoice in God's plan. For many years I had the joy of leading a group of women in a bible study at a local community center. The neutral location drew some who might not have joined us otherwise. We became a true "circle of friends" from a variety of church backgrounds, ages, life experiences, and faith walks. With my return to teaching, I can no longer lead that group. But I am trusting God to call and equip new leaders so the ministry can continue to bless many.

Confusion is bound to be a part of your experience as the parent of a prodigal. Seek godly counsel and stay connected to God in prayer. Do the best you can to guide your prodigal and try to keep your thoughts from racing too far into the future. Choices may seem to cause permanent problems, but withhold your judgment for a few years. In time, the dust will settle, the clouds will lift, and the Redeemer will amaze you by using it all, even the pain, for His glory. I can't explain how He does it, but I'm eternally grateful He does. Do not allow confusion to shred your faith.

During times of confusion it is important to stay connected to your prodigal. Mark Gregston's book, *When Your Teen is Struggling*, is an excellent resource. He says, "If you are feeling miserable in the midst of the struggle you're going through, I can guarantee your child feels worse. This is the time they need your presence, your guidance, and your heart." My relationship today with both Mindy and Danny is sweet and blessed. We went through the storm of confusion together, and that has made all the difference.

For Personal Reflection

1. How long have you been traveling this road with your prodigal? Has it become more or less confusing along the way? Why?

2. What avenues have your explored to find support and guidance during this time?

3. Describe a time in your life when God made sense out of a confusing situation.

4. Write out some of the questions that are burdening you at this point in the journey.

Pray: Ask for God's wisdom to bring order out of any ongoing chaos in your home. Reaffirm your trust in His power to lead, guide, and heal.

CHAPTER FOUR

GUILT

Basic question: What did I do wrong?
Why wasn't I a better parent?
Heart string: Satan is the accuser; God understands,
forgives and restores.

In my experience, the most devastating emotion to deal with is guilt. As I picture an arsenal of arrows ready and aimed at my heart by the enemy, the majority of them are arrows of guilt. It is so natural to blame ourselves when our child rebels. "If only" thoughts are like quicksand, pulling us downward in despair.

As a bible study leader and retreat speaker, I have done much self-evaluation related to whether or not to keep teaching in the midst of heartbreak. There are some who would advise a rest from ministry because of genuine concern for my well-being. Others cast a judging eye my way and would have me keep silent because of perceived "failure". In *Facing the Giants in Your Life*, Dr. David Jeremiah says, "By studying our failures, we will discover what we are doing wrong which can only lead us more quickly to what to do right. Failure is an event, not a person; failure is something that happens, not someone you become." The guilt we feel when we recognize mistakes in our parenting should lead us to the Lord who stands ready to forgive.

Beware of another kind of guilt that is not healthy but an arrow from the accuser. Dr. Jeremiah explains, "True guilt is a God-given emotion to actual sin; false guilt is a conditioned response with no basis in fact. When feeling guilty, deciding whether the guilt is true or false is the first step to being free." Let God be the One to lead you to repent when necessary and to set you free to serve Him when He calls.

In fact, God most often uses broken vessels for His work. A life-changing bible study for me years ago was Donna Partow's, *Becoming A Vessel God Can Use*. May she encourage your heart as she did mine with these words, "As a follower of Jesus Christ, you have been called by God for a very specific purpose. Not to live out a perfect life in your own perfect little corner of the world, but to come alongside imperfect people suffering the inevitable pain of living in an imperfect world . . . Following Jesus isn't about rules and perfection; it's about forgiveness and grace. We are 'called alongside to help.'" Amen!

> Recently God amazed me with a ministry opportunity right in the middle of a troubling time with Mindy. I was driving to a Dove Singers performance, preparing my heart and mind to sing with this precious group of believers about

the power of the cross. The cell phone rang and I answered. "Is this Nancy?" "Yes, it is". "This is the director of Camp Berea, and I'm calling to ask if you're available to speak at our upcoming Mother Daughter Retreat." Details followed as I struggled to stay focused. My heart was racing because of all that was going on with my precious daughter at the time. I felt like such a failure as a mother and was second-guessing so many things. Yet here was an open door right in the area of my pain. "Surely they won't want me," I said to myself sadly and then began to speak. "Thank you so much for inviting me, but please know I am in the midst of some serious problems with my one and only daughter . . ." My eyes were getting warm with tears and I expected the call would end abruptly. But this man was a grace-giver and he listened with care and concern. "Let's just pray about it for a few days," he replied, "and see how God leads." Grace came from a godly stranger, but it was accompanied by a barrage of arrows from the enemy.

We are players in the games of our prodigals. At times we may even be instigators of bad decisions. We say the wrong thing. We let things go unpunished. We make too much of a small offense. We are preoccupied and miss teachable moments. We succumb to their tactics to wear us down. We respond inappropriately. Yes, that all happens. But we are not ultimately responsible for their wrong choices. Let that be a freeing truth for you! Since repetition is good, let me say this once more directly to you. *You are not ultimately responsible for anyone's wrong choices!* Your life need not be consumed with guilt regarding theirs. Refuse to let false guilt isolate you and destroy your life. Honestly take responsibility for your missteps. Confess and then receive God's forgiveness. Take another step closer to Him and let Him redeem you. Be amazed as He leads you forward to serve others.

> As I slept the night following the conversation with the Camp Director, I was restless and awake in the early morning hours. But I remember it now with great joy and amazement. God was flooding my mind with ideas about what to teach at that retreat, along with visual aids and even a take-home reminder for each attendee. I raced to my computer to capture the overflowing thoughts. A few weeks later, I enjoyed a rich, wonderful weekend as God used my brokenness to touch the hearts of others. Thank you, Lord, for grace-givers! Thank You for being the ultimate Grace-Giver.

Guilt will come, but we must overcome those thoughts in the strength of our Savior. None of us will parent perfectly. We will all make mistakes and fall short. How dangerous it is when we become so performance-based in our judgments. Parents often take credit for "successful" children and wonder why everyone else is having problems. Many who have not experienced a prodigal can be insensitive and over-confident in their own abilities. Even innocent comments can awaken guilt in the heart of a hurting parent. We struggle with our seeming ineffectiveness compared to what others are experiencing.

At those times it helps me to remember even *God's* children don't always behave! He is the perfect Parent, and yet His children make wrong choices every day. That is a glaring reminder to me that *even if I had parented perfectly*, there would still be problems. This world is infected with sin and that impacts us all.

Let these words from Hebrews 10:22-23 wash over you:

> "Let us draw near to God with a sincere heart in full assurance of faith, having our hearts sprinkled to cleanse us from a guilty conscience and having our bodies washed with pure water. Let us hold unswervingly to the hope we profess for He who promised is faithful."

For Personal Reflection

1. What are some arrows of guilt you have felt from the enemy related to your prodigal?

2. Have you been set free yet by the truth that *you are not responsible* for your prodigal's wrong choices? How would you explain this truth to another parent experiencing guilt?

3. List three ways you have witnessed God's faithfulness to you during your lifetime.

Pray: Turn again to the Lord for reassurance, forgiveness, and renewed joy. Let Him cleanse you from a guilty conscience and restore your trust in His faithfulness.

CHAPTER FIVE

SORROW

Basic question: How did it get to this point?
Heart string: God is with me and
He will wipe away my tears.

How many tears have been shed over prodigals? How many hearts have been ripped to shreds because of the sorrow of seeing a beloved child slip away? I can't even write this chapter without dissolving into tears. The sorrow is real and must be addressed, but we should not linger any more than necessary. Heartbreak is unavoidable for the parent of a prodigal. Scenes come to mind years later, capturing the sorrow like worn photographs. My photo album includes:

- Riding behind the ambulance one night on the way to a psychiatric hospital. The light inside revealed my child on the stretcher as I watched her through the back window. Praise music was playing in my car and Graham Kendrick ushered me before the throne of God so that I could endure that drive.

- The White Mountains of New Hampshire were the backdrop for numerous trips to the girls' shelter where Mindy spent many months in an attempt to get her focused and back on track. I can still picture the amazing beauty of the surroundings that softened the harsh reality of leaving my child behind.

- A metal telephone pole hardly showing the impact of my son's car the night before. Thankfully, he was spared serious injury and noted later that the metal pole probably saved his life since a wooden pole could have snapped and destroyed both he and his car.

- Four holes in the family room wall from my son's fist. I saw it happen and then lived for months with the vivid reminder of my son's rage. What had happened to my precious little boy?

There are other scenes not appropriate to share without revealing more details than necessary. Fortunately, my children have thus far escaped serious physical injury. However, I have dear friends whose sorrow extends to the depths of the grave. The reality is that some prodigals do not return home in this life. Some are taken home to heaven and received by their loving, forgiving heavenly Father. I am comforted in knowing that my prodigals have made a personal profession of faith in Jesus Christ, securing for them the eternal home prepared by Him in the event of their death. I do have another beloved son in heaven. He was taken home as an infant following a full-term pregnancy. Yet even that sorrow has been tempered with the hope of heaven and the confidence that he is with Jesus where we will one day be reunited. (see my first book, *"Where is My Baby? . . . a mother's message of hope and healing"*)

Recall these comforting words from Psalm 23:4: "Even though I walk through the valley of the shadow of death, I will fear no evil for You are with me. Your rod and Your staff, they comfort me." Sorrow comes from living in the valley where the shadow of death looms everywhere. We recognize those shadows and understand the dangers facing our prodigals more clearly than they. We anticipate the long-term consequences of their poor choices. We dream of what might have been.

All parents have high expectations for their children. We want them to be successful in school, to make good friends, and to find a fulfilling career. Many desire to see their child serving the Lord and growing in relationship with Him, finding God's choice for a spouse, and one day becoming a godly, caring parent. When our prodigal marches off the path in defiance and lingers on the road to rebellion, those dreams are seriously threatened. Our hearts can be overwhelmed with sorrow because things are not going according to plan.

So how can you deal with heartbreaking sorrow? First, remember God hears your cries and cares about your tears. He knows the details of your situation and you can turn to Him without having to explain your every heartache. Find comfort and strength in

His presence. Second, be open and honest with your spouse or a close friend. Admit your fears and receive the healing balm of encouragement. Third, avoid being in the company of those who are negative and discouraging. Surround yourself with people who care and provide positive, godly encouragement.

Fourth, do not be consumed by your sorrows. Find other outlets where you can be refreshed and see a different side of life. Refuse to let your focus be narrowed by your sorrows. Find the beauty in each new day. Small things serve as reminders of God's love and can bring joy during the darkest days. I especially love my *Really Woolly* sheep that decorate my desk. One has his hands folded in prayer with a bible under his arm, another is a shepherd, and a third is a shepherd holding a little lamb. I love to think of Jesus as my loving, caring Shepherd, leading me on the path of life and preparing the way. I often picture myself as the little lamb in His strong arms. Another joy for me is seeing budding trees and blooming flowers, amazing reminders of the promise of new life. Hearing a special song with rich, godly lyrics can propel me out of the pit and into God's presence. You'll need to find some things that restore the joy in your life, for as it says in the bible:

> "Weeping may remain for a night, but rejoicing comes in the morning." (Psalm 30:5b)

> "Do not grieve, for the joy of the Lord is your strength." (Nehemiah 8:10b)

"My flesh and my heart may fail, but God is the
strength of my heart and my portion forever."
(Psalm 73:26)

It may also be appropriate to speak to a Christ-focused counselor
about your sorrow if it lingers too long. Depression is real and
could be triggered by many of the emotions that come with
being the parent of a prodigal. Beware that the guilt, sorrow
and shame can become crushing and tempt you to retreat from
life. Heed these powerful words from Phil Waldrep, author of
Parenting Prodigals: "Most of us have prayed for years that God
would change our prodigals. Perhaps we need to pray that God
will change us first . . . Our prodigals surely need the touch of
God, but perhaps we need to feel it first. Then, as God works His
kindness and healing in our hearts, our faces and our words can
better reflect God's love to our prodigals and to everyone else
around us." Bring your sorrow to the Lord for He is the One who
is able to comfort and restore you.

FOR PERSONAL REFLECTION

1. What are some life experiences that have brought you great sorrow?

2. Have you been able to keep moving forward on the journey of life, one step at a time? What do you believe is your next step?

3. Who is a trusted friend to whom you can turn for encouragement?

4. List some little things that bring you joy even in the midst of troubling times.

Pray: Imagine that you are the little lamb in the arms of the Shepherd and rest for a few minutes in His comforting presence. What is He softly saying to you?

Chapter Six

Shame

Basic question: What will others think?
How can I face my friends?
Heart string: Seek to please God and not other people.

Shame was not one of the emotions that lingered for me. But when it came, it came like a flood. I can only remember three occasions as I look back over the years. The first was especially hurtful because it came from such an unexpected place.

As women's ministries director I had many opportunities to interact with women. I love the one-on-one times, but especially thrive on teaching God's word to groups. My style is to be as transparent as possible because I want women to know I am a fellow-struggler on the path of life. I do not teach because I have it all together. Instead, I teach because I know firsthand the power of God to propel us through the darkness into the Light! At that time, God was opening more and more doors for me to teach in other locations and it was the joy of my life to proclaim Christ's redemptive power wherever I went. Yet, a well-meaning pastor and his wife confronted me one day in his office. They began by describing their successful, wonderful daughter (an only child) and noted that I was having some problems with my own daughter. They were suggesting I focus more time and energy on my home and less on ministry. Was I really hearing this correctly? Were they taking credit for their daughter's choices and blaming me for those of my child? While I understand in retrospect their genuine concern, my child was not making destructive choices because she was neglected at home. I believed my home and family were well cared for. Unable to maintain composure, I dissolved into tears and felt shame I had never known.

There are certainly times in ministry when we need to pull back to focus on our families. My pastor deserved my respect and his observations carried authority because of his position over me. Yet, God did not personally confirm that rebuke. He continued to lead me forward with gentleness and affirmation. My family was supportive and close friends understood that ministry was truly my God-given life-line.

Because of my teaching responsibilities, I spent extra time in prayer and received rich nourishment from God's life-giving Word. On some occasions, Mindy traveled with me for speaking events. She saw and heard me proclaim God's faithfulness, knowing more details about my life than anyone else in the room. She knew the struggles and witnessed firsthand the power of God to use a broken vessel like me. Those rides home provided an unusually fertile atmosphere for discussing spiritual things.

So, when shame reared its ugly head that first time, I chose to trust my Shepherd. In retrospect, I'm still convinced it was the right decision to continue in ministry. How risky for anyone to presume to know God's will for someone else. Listen for God's voice as He leads you personally and powerfully along the path He has chosen.

Recently I heard a favorite bible teacher, James MacDonald, affirm that when we go through trials we *should* keep on serving the Lord with our gifts. Problems and imperfections do not disqualify us from serving God. Yet the enemy loves to use shame in an attempt to silence us. My new church home is led by a pastor who understands and supports me. I am so thankful for him and for others who have been my cheerleaders.

> As I drove down Pinkerton hill one morning I saw the high school students rustling about to get to class. The young girls reminded me of Mindy—dressed provocatively like she was prone to do, hair in the latest style. But Mindy was not there as she should have been. She had

violated probation multiple times and was living at a girls' home hours away. Her weekend visits were disappointing because she was so unhappy, so bent on breaking the rules and contacting her risky circle of friends.

My mind raced to the previous Sunday morning when she had a hard time sitting in the church service. I remembered her dark makeup and her restlessness. She felt out of place and left after only a few minutes. These high school girls were doing what they needed to do. They probably had struggles, but their lives were moving along in the *right* direction. That's when pride got the best of me and shame reared its ugly head.

"Oh Lord," I said in my heart, "why is my daughter so messed up? It is embarrassing for me sometimes. Everyone at church knows that I'm a bible teacher and many have been in my classes. Yet my own daughter is so visibly rebellious and on a path of destruction." In a moment God responded with one word that clearly resounded in my self-centered heart. He spoke deep within my spirit, "Hosea".

Tears came flooding in as I realized God was reminding me of the story of Hosea and his harlot wife. God deliberately chose an unfaithful wife for Hosea and then gave him the assignment to love and forgive her as a picture of His love and forgiveness for the nation of Israel. Mindy is mine to love and forgive. She is *my special gift* to show forth the grace of God. My prideful shame was smashed upon the altar in God's heavenly throne room and replaced with a supernatural love for my daughter. No longer an embarrassment to me, Mindy is my treasure and I am her #1 fan. *Everyone* needs a cheerleader.

Shame is never from God. It is a fingerprint of the enemy and needs to be destroyed. Jesus took our shame when He willingly gave His life for us on the cross. If your prodigal is bringing you shame, allow God to transform it so that His unconditional love can fill you to overflowing. While we don't condone sin, we must be sure to love the sinner.

Danny was a different kind of prodigal. He sinned with a smile. He charmed his way into my heart and didn't resort to foul language with me or disrespect. It is hard to recall feeling shame over his misdeeds, except for that one night. Well, to be honest, there were a few nights. I was awakened around 3 in the morning from a sound sleep by a nudge from God. He was preparing me

to be ready for the phone call that came within
minutes.

Danny was stranded and needed a ride home.
Somehow he had ended up at a nearby movie
theater, without his car and without his jacket.
It was wintertime and he was freezing cold. I
left quickly and drove through the parking lot
looking for my prodigal. I spotted him near a
police car and pulled up nearby. He got in, closed
the door, and thanked me for coming. If I hadn't,
he would have spent the night in jail. I caught
the eye of the police officer and wondered what
he was thinking. Shame rushed in for a moment
because no doubt he was judging me, along with
my wayward son.

We got home, Danny went upstairs to bed, and
I tried to get back to sleep. It felt good to come
to the rescue. It felt better to know he was home
safe. But the enemy never sleeps. He whispered
condemnation to my soul once again, "You are
such a sad excuse for a mother. Why didn't you
let him spend the night in jail? He doesn't deserve
being rescued. That policeman thinks you are a
fool." The arrow stung for a moment, but God's
peace overruled in my heart. I pictured myself
and Danny in the shelter of God's wings and the

arrows of shame and condemnation bounced off my shield of faith, powerless. *Praise God from whom all blessings flow!*

We are so prone to live to please men, rather than God. We care about everyone's opinion and seek approval, even from strangers. The dictionary defines shame as "the painful feeling arising from the consciousness of something dishonorable, improper, ridiculous done by oneself or another." (dictionary.com) There is pain when we consider the improper and often ridiculous deeds of our prodigal. But shame is not God's desire for His own. He wants to deliver us from shame as we seek Him and turn to Him for protection and healing.

Mark Gregston wisely says, "This struggle has come to your family for a reason. You're the parent of *this* child for a reason. The timing is not accidental. You probably don't understand all the reasons, but that doesn't diminish their purpose or the plan behind them. They are part of the journey God has for you and your child. And He'll use it all." I believe this with my whole heart. Without Danny and Mindy my life would be incomplete. It is my joy and privilege to be their mother. God continues to be my refuge and strength and I treasure these promises from Psalm 34:4-5, 8:

"I sought the Lord, and He answered me; He delivered me from all my fears.

Those who look to Him are radiant; their faces are never covered with shame.

Taste and see that the Lord is good; blessed is the man who takes refuge in Him."

FOR PERSONAL REFLECTION

1. What specific things have brought you shame concerning your prodigal?

2. How does the reminder about Hosea speak to your heart?

3. Who has been a cheerleader for you during your lifetime? Who will be a cheerleader for your prodigal, if not you?

Pray: Spend time in prayer confessing any prideful shame about what others may think of your situation. Ask God to surround you with His healing presence.

CHAPTER SEVEN

FRUSTRATION

Basic question: What can I do to stop this?
Heart string: Apart from Him I can do absolutely nothing.
My job is to abide in Christ.

"Enough is enough!" Have you gotten to this point yet? "The madness and chaos have to stop. There must be *something* I can do to put an end to this!" Depending on how long you have been living with a prodigal, your frustration level could very well be hitting the ceiling. I was frustrated early in the process because I thought the situation could be turned around with good, solid reason. My words fell empty on the floor and my attempts to "enlighten" were futile.

Time is a necessary ingredient in the process of maturity. You will recall in the parable Jesus told about the prodigal son, it took time for the son to come to a place of brokenness and true repentance. He had to spend some time in the pig pen before he desired to be reconciled with his father. Waldrep reminds us, "Self-discovery is a very lonely and difficult course, but for most prodigals, it is the only path back. No one else can help them until they are ready to face some harsh realities."

Danny started on the rebel road when he was about seventeen. It has been eight-plus years since then, and he has come through with relatively few scars. His struggles continued during that time as the strongholds changed. He had moments of deep reflection and times of crushing discouragement. Through it all, he had an awareness the Father was watching over him and every so often, he let me know.

> Sitting at the kitchen table one day, I saw in Danny an openness to talk. Sometimes it was drug-induced, but this time was different. He was on a better path and had experienced some freedom from the bondage gripping him for so long. I wanted to give him a chance to share his feelings, so I resisted the urge to engage in a monologue praising his recent victories. I took a deep breath and simply said, "So, how have you been doing?" "Good, Mom. I'm really doing better." His tone was calm and sincere. I continued the probe, "Well, what do you think is the reason for the turn-around?" He looked at me with a puzzled expression as if I should have known the answer. Indeed, I should have! But it was so healing when it came from his lips. "Mommm . . . the Lord." I nearly fell off my chair. My son was acknowledging

the fundamental truth I had prayed so long he would grasp.

The Lord is the One who changes lives. He is the One who sets us free. But His timetable is beyond our understanding. His ways are not our ways, as the scripture affirms. He cares about the process, not just the end result. The twists and turns, the closed doors, the U-turns, the steep slopes cause frustration for the frail of heart. My prodigals have had so many "ups" and "downs" over the years and I never did enjoy roller coaster rides!

Sometimes frustration is related to a perceived promise from the Lord that is delayed. For example, how many times have you thought of that verse in Proverbs 22:6 that says, "Train up a child in the way he should go, and when he is old he will not depart from it."? When we have done all we know to do and the results are not as "promised", this can be breeding ground for frustration. But the Proverbs are not to be read as firm promises. They are general statements about what is likely. Waldrep helps to clarify with these hope-filled thoughts, "If a child is exposed to the ways and the truth of God when he is young, those messages will stay in his heart for the rest of his life. Though his choices and behavior may take him far from God, the truth of God stays lodged in his mind. So Proverbs 22:6 is not a promise that the child will never depart from God's path, but instead it reminds us that God's message remains rooted in that person's life and cannot be eradicated."

Mindy was attending a youth group at another church. Her rebellion was causing problems and the day came when I was asked to meet with one of the adult leaders. The scene was devastating to me. The words and actions of my daughter at the meeting shocked me. Frustration is a mild word for the emotions I felt. It was tempting to just throw my hands up in defeat and disengage. Surely, she was beyond my ability to parent. I recently found a letter dated 6/5/07, written the day following this episode. Evidently I had let the frustration get the best of me and I spoke sharply to her on the ride home. I can't recall what I said, but the letter begins with an apology:

"Dear Mindy,

I am writing to apologize for losing it with you on the ride home yesterday. I shouldn't have said some of the things I did – In fact, I can't even remember what I said but I'm sure you can. Please forgive me for anything that was hurtful. It all came out in a moment of frustration and fear. I was frustrated because you didn't seem to feel at all sorry for behaving the way you did at the meeting . . . and I was fearful of what you might do – like run away again . . . and again.

Please know that my love for you isn't based on whether or not I am "happy with you" at the moment. There will be times when I get angry, but that doesn't mean I don't love you. I am always concerned for you – your well-being, your safety, your future . . . You mean the world to me and my greatest joy will be seeing you 'all grown up' and happy. That is my hope . . .

But in the meantime, let me just review some things I may have neglected to teach you. Repetition is good – so if you've heard it before, 'humor me' and read through it anyways . . ."

I went on to express thoughts about respect, compliance, selfishness, and getting serious with the Lord and then concluded the letter:

"I'm not sure if you'll read this with an open mind. I hope you're not furious with me for saying these things. My goal is to help you. I know God is able to help us during this shaky time. I know He loves you and He is fighting evil forces for you. He won't give up and neither will I. I am here for you. I love you and I am praying for you.

Love,
Mom xxoo"

Are you at a point of frustration? Wait. Stay connected to God and to your child. Do everything you can to hang in there. Scatter the seed of the Word when appropriate and refuse to withdraw or disengage. Gregston warns, "If parents abandon children during a time of difficulty or bad behavior, who will help them process the way they think about who they are during a time of struggle? If you pull out emotionally during this time, how will your kids ever learn about God's grace, His acceptance, or His love?"

You might try writing a letter to your prodigal. It is a way to give them something to read at their leisure without the pressure of confrontation. Be sure to include words of love and acceptance, but don't back away from expressing your frustration. Speak the truth in love. If you have something for which to apologize, do that too.

For Personal Reflection

1. What causes you the most frustration related to your prodigal?

2. In what ways have you scattered good seed into the heart of your child?

3. What evidence have you seen that your prodigal is aware of God's hand upon them?

Pray: Ask God for wisdom about writing a letter to your prodigal. Allow the Holy Spirit to show you anything for which you need to apologize. Listen as the Lord speaks His truth to your heart and reminds you of His unfailing love.

ANGER

Basic question: How could he do this to me and to himself?
Heart string: God wants me to forgive and stands ready
to diffuse the entire situation.

In a recent bible study, we considered the topic of anger. Being angry is not a sin; the problem comes when we express our anger in unhealthy ways. In a world full of injustice, crime, abuse, and neglect, anger is often an appropriate emotion. Sin *should* make us angry because it is a blot upon God's perfectly created world. If you have experienced the forceful emotion of anger related to the deeds of your prodigal, you may well be justified. The challenge is to get rid of it before it does any damage. The spark needs to be put out before a consuming fire emerges.

> The first time Mindy ran away was a few years ago when she was in her first long-term placement. Looking back, it was a "cushy" opportunity for her to get things in order. She had a lovely room in a beautifully restored old home, access to shopping and a nearby gym under supervision,

and bus rides to and from her hometown high school. I visited often and remember sitting on the large veranda, near a lovely park. Yet one day, after getting off the bus at school, she bolted. She was gone for a few weeks, as I recall. I was devastated and worried for her safety. The local newspaper printed an article with her picture and many were praying for her with deep love and concern. Then I got the call.

"Mindy?" I asked excitedly, "Is this really you? Where are you? Are you OK?" The questions were streaming out as I tried to remain calm. "Yes, it's me," she said tearfully. "I'm OK. I want to come home. Will you please come and get me?" "Of course! Where?" I could hardly breathe. She replied, "At the mall in Salem. Come to the food court." I hung up and raced to my car. The drive seemed to take an eternity as I called my mother and my sister to tell them that Mindy was OK (yes, on my cell phone which was legal at the time). I hadn't been to that mall very often and tried to remember what entrance was near the food court. I called my son for directions and then raced up the stairway to the food court. I can still picture it in my mind – so many windows – so much light – so much hope. During the entire ride I had tried to imagine the moment when I would embrace my daughter with tears of relief.

But it was not to be. She was nowhere in that food court. I walked around many times during the hour and a half I was there. I prayed and waited for my cell phone to ring with her explanation. No Mindy. No call. No embrace. Then the dread came as I imagined all sorts of terrible scenarios. The ride home was solemn and tearful. I rushed over to see if the home phone had a message, but there was no relief there. So I went upstairs and something led me to her room. In shock I realized some of her clothes were gone. The anger was welling up as I kept pushing away the thought she had tricked me. But when I went into my son's room across the hall, the reality sunk in like a brick. His game system was gone! She had lured me away from the house in order to come in to steal from us.

What do you do with that kind of betrayal and anger? I don't remember much of what happened next, but by God's grace, He removed the sting of anger in me before it could do severe damage. Dr. David Jeremiah says, "When we choose not to get rid of our anger, the danger is that it will become something worse. Anger turns into resentment, and resentment turns into bitterness, and bitterness turns into unforgiveness, and unforgiveness turns into a defiled conscience. Pretty soon, we have become captives of our own anger." The police eventually found Mindy and the journey of rebellion continued for many more months. But she knew my love for her remained intact, even after this horrifying episode of betrayal.

Please understand. I did express anger during those prodigal years. I wasn't always able to put out the ember before it fanned into flame. In fact, the worst outburst of anger came fairly recently and it wasn't directed toward either of my prodigals.

It was 2 in the morning and I couldn't sleep. So many thoughts were swirling around in my head – angry thoughts. We had been in juvenile court for the final time that day. Mindy had been found from another run and was ready to leave temporary shelter. Her 18th birthday was less than two months away and I was desperate to get her help. Someone had recommended a treatment program nearby and I made many phone calls to prepare the way for Mindy to go there. But in a surprise turn at court that day, the judge dismissed her case and sent her home! The juvenile probation officer was giving up on her, in my opinion, saying, "we've done all we can." In my mind, that just didn't ring true. This final opportunity for help remained, but it was tossed aside mainly because of her coming birthday. I may never understand why. Couldn't two months of treatment be helpful? How can I bring her home the way she is?

Throughout the nearly two years of court and probation dealings, I had always admired and appreciated the help from the judge and probation officer. But at this juncture, I felt betrayed and left to fend for myself. I was alone, angry, and scared. So in the early morning hours I crafted an email, filled with my anger and pain, and clicked to send it in an instant to the JPPO (Juvenile Probation and Parole Officer). May she forgive me. Yet, my fears *did* prove true since the coming two months would prove to be the worst ever.

In reflecting upon my anger related to my prodigals, there are relatively few occasions that come to mind. I often tell my bible study groups that God has blessed me with the gift of forgetfulness. The worst moments seem to be taken away from memory and for that, I am deeply thankful. Both Danny and Mindy had friends along the way who were magnets for my anger. I also remember being angry with a youth pastor who seemed unwilling to come alongside Danny in those early years. Yet in each situation, forgiveness has released me from the quicksand of bitterness.

In *Facing Your Feelings*, Vickie Kraft writes "If we won't forgive, bitterness will become firmly entrenched in our characters. It will make us cynical, unable to trust, and unable to maintain close relationships. On the other hand, forgiveness will free us to go on in peace, unhindered in our enjoyment of the Lord." The basis for our forgiveness is the cross of Christ. When we receive God's grace through faith and trust in Christ's sacrificial death on our behalf, we are forgiven of all sin: past, present, and future. Jesus instructs us to likewise, release others from our anger by forgiving them.

Sometimes I've wanted to hold on to anger, but God seems to remove it supernaturally from my heart. I have a note I was passing back and forth with Mindy in church one Sunday.

> The specifics elude me, but I recall Mindy had tried my patience once again. As she sat next to me in church that day, I was overcome with unexplainable love and forgiveness that the Holy Spirit was pouring into my heart. I wrote, "I should be so angry with you right now, but all I feel is an overwhelming love for you." She read it, smiled, and leaned forward as my signal to scratch her back. It was a special moment. So simple, but so profound.

Mark Gregston runs Heartlight Ministries, a residential counseling facility for troubled teens. He is often asked why their program is so effective. His answer: "We love kids when they're at their worst. I haven't met a teen yet who doesn't want to know he or she will continue to be loved when everything is a mess. The first thing to do is to move toward your kids, especially if they are struggling and in a tough spot. Tell them at least every week that you love them, not because of what they do but because of who they are."

Instead of harboring angry thoughts and memories, release them to the One who can bring healing. Allow God to diffuse your anger into forgiveness. He is able to bring reconciliation to any situation. It is right to be angry about the sin and to carry out reasonable consequences, but grace and forgiveness must be extended to the sinner. More wisdom from Gregston, "If you show love to your prodigal, you may catch flak from the 'Pharisees' in your church. But if you recall, that was the very reason Jesus told the parable of the Prodigal Son. He wanted to show the rigid, self-righteous religious contingent that God's heart was big enough to forgive *even sinners.* The risk of loving is always a risk worth taking." Let God's unfailing love for you become a catalyst for radical healing in your relationship with your prodigal.

FOR PERSONAL REFLECTION

1. Describe a time when you felt angry about something related to your prodigal.

2. How easy is it for you to forgive? What might be hindering the process?

3. What do you do when you get angry? Is there anything you might try to do differently next time?

Pray: Give the Holy Spirit freedom to expose any anger or unforgiveness in you that needs to be uprooted. Surrender to Him and choose to extend forgiveness where needed.

Chapter Nine

Release

Basic question: Where can I put my trust and find rest?
Heart string: God is good and wise and loving toward all
He has made; He is worthy of my complete trust;
He is watching over my child in love.

Daily life with a prodigal is unpredictable. Some days are relatively routine, but a storm is always brewing. I have seen things change from calm to chaos in an instant. In the racing winds of those storms, we need a safe place to land. Sometimes the emotional, spiritual, and physical toll seems more than we can handle. In dealing with my prodigals, there were days when I was exhausted, inside and out. Sadly, the relationship with my husband had broken down and he was not living at home during most of the difficult years. Without his love and support, the burden became quite heavy at times. If you have a spouse to lean on, be thankful and allow each trial to draw you closer to one another and to God.

The bible has such wonderful promises to cling to in the storms of life. Here are just a few of my favorite:

"He knows the way that I take; when He has tested me, I will come forth as gold." (Job 23:10)

"Trust in the Lord with all your heart and lean not on your own understanding; in all your ways acknowledge Him, and He will make your paths straight." (Proverbs 3:5-6)

"Our light and momentary troubles are achieving for us an eternal glory that far outweighs them all. So we fix our eyes not on what is seen, but on what is unseen. For what is seen is temporary, but what is unseen is eternal." (2 Cor. 4:17-18)

"He who dwells in the shelter of the Most High will rest in the shadow of the Almighty . . . He will cover you with His feathers and under His wings you will find refuge; His faithfulness will be your shield and rampart." (Psalm 91:1, 4)

God is my safe place to land whenever strong winds begin to stir. I often imagine myself held safely and lovingly in His strong arms or covered by His protective wings. When there is nobody who truly understands, God is waiting. When the bottom falls out, He is there to catch you before you fall. These truths are no longer clichés to me for I know their power firsthand.

Most parents of prodigals will agree that in all the pain and uncertainty, our prayer lives develop in new ways. Initially I prayed fervently for my prodigal, suggesting such great ideas to God about how to fix the problem. "O Lord, please take care of Mindy by . . ." "Lord, Danny needs to . . . so if You could just do this . . ." Well, He rarely took my advice. Then I would pray for protection and remind God about all the possible dangers lurking along the path of my prodigal. Other times I would pray for all the people influencing my prodigal and ask God to remove some and send in others for the rescue. It was like a game of Stratego. I felt such responsibility to pray the right prayers, to think of everything, to put together a great plan, but my strategies were usually not heeded. God was being so patient with me, and I needed to learn that He was the One in charge, not me.

John Ortberg's book, *When the Game is Over, It All Goes Back in the Box*, describes God as the Master of the Board. One of the chapters is dedicated to explaining how to resign as Master of the Board and leave that role to God. He writes, "If I have surrendered, if I have put God in control, then I can release all outcomes. I don't have to carry the weight of the world anymore. I can be open to face each day with a sense of wonder, gratitude, freedom, relaxation, and delight." This truth applies to every area of life. In parenting prodigals, we need perspective and release. We truly don't have to carry the weight of the world anymore.

There are two aspects of release to consider. First, release involves refusing to rescue; to allow your prodigal to experience the consequences of bad choices. Gregston cites Proverbs 19:18, "Discipline your son for in that there is hope; do not be a willing party to his death." He says, "I believe God is encouraging us as parents to allow pain in our children's lives to help set the boundaries of choices, and to let consequences have their full impact in order to help our children heed the warning: Don't go there." Parents who constantly jump in to fix a prodigal's problems might actually block God's redemptive work and hinder what is needed for redemption and change. My prayer time now often includes the phrase, "Lord, please don't let me get in the way of what You need to do."

Secondly, forgiveness is deeply connected to release. Perhaps it has been your pattern to constantly remind your prodigal of your dissatisfaction with his choices. In thinking that the reminders will shame him into reform, your repetition of his faults may be causing deep pain. Waldrep writes, "Every parent of a prodigal can come up with plenty of reasons to feel hurt and angry at their son or daughter. But we need to move beyond those things and focus on sources of healing, love, and grace – first for ourselves, and then for our children who are desperate for our unconditional acceptance." The power of the cross reminds me that we are all sinners in need of a Savior. Instead of repeatedly underscoring your prodigal's mistakes, consider that your words can be like sandpaper, causing deep and unintentional wounding. Our words must be chosen carefully and seasoned with love.

The long drive through the White Mountains was breathtakingly beautiful, but somber. Mindy was expected today at Davenport, a long-term placement home for girls. Conversation was never a problem for us, but on this ride Mindy was quieter than usual. Her music was playing loudly as she began to withdraw and nap frequently along the way. I continued my ongoing conversation with the Lord. "I can't believe this is happening, Lord. Do I really have to leave my daughter at this place so far away? How will I ever be able to say 'goodbye'? What is going to happen to her? Will she find caring, supportive people or will she be treated harshly?" Though I didn't hear an audible reply, I knew God was saying, "Keep driving. Move forward and trust Me. *I will* take care of her."

I glanced over at Mindy often as she napped. She was so beautiful in my eyes. She had so much potential. How did we ever end up in this place? My tears were falling, but she didn't see. I was trying so hard to stay positive and strong. Mindy's choices had led to this day and I needed to follow through and let her face these consequences.

The staff who greeted us when we arrived was friendly enough. The place was rustic, but welcoming. It took hours for the intake process, but it was all a blur. So many forms to be signed, questions to be answered, people to meet, belongings to be inventoried, hugs to be given. "I love you, Mindy. I'll be back soon to see you. Call me. I'll be praying for you." I was barely able to maintain emotional control. On the way back home, alone, the struggle within continued. "O God, how can this be happening?!?! My daughter! My precious daughter! It hurts so badly." The tears were making it hard to focus so I pulled off the road to grab tissues and recover. That was a true turning point. The Holy Spirit ministered to my spirit and gave me a calmness and peace that was beyond my understanding. It was my moment of surrender – my daughter, my control, my plans. I let out a deep breath and spoke, "Lord, I *will* trust You. This feels awful, but You haven't left either of us alone. You love Mindy even more than I do, and *I trust You* to protect her and be with her on this new journey." Release! In a strange way, it felt good.

Imagine holding a ragged rock in clenched fist. Squeeze tightly and hold that position for a long time. Then gradually open your hand and set the rock free. Doesn't it brings such relief when we let go? As I drove home that day, I began to experience some badly-needed emotional relief. I wouldn't have to lock up valuables or worry constantly about where Mindy was and what she was doing. Someone else would be directing her every move and helping to shape the direction of her life. I didn't rescue Mindy, but let her face the harsh consequences of her months of poor choices. The outcome was not mine to control. I had resigned as Master of the Board.

Only a few days after God's powerful lesson of release and surrender, He gave me these words as I continued to embrace His grace-gift of rest and release:

From Squirming to Silence

The valley of the shadows is a place where many dwell.
It's filled with thoughts and longings for a time when all was well.
Bad choices, wasted moments interfere with our ideal—
We cling to dreams unspoken—turn away from what is real.

Denial and regret cause such turmoil in our minds.
If only life could stop for just a moment to rewind.
Would I choose to live life differently or did I stay on track?
I can recall some choices that I wish I could take back.

Life's daily struggles clamor for the place of center stage.
Emptiness and worry are the watchwords of this Age.
The things I care most deeply for aren't shared by those I love;
So few have thoughts at all about the God who dwells above.

The enemy hurls painful darts at weak points in my life.
He tells me I have failed as both a mother and a wife.
Yet there behind the sorrow is a sense of meaning still—
As I cling to my life's passion to stand firm inside God's will.

Against those darts of doubt and fear, I'll hold my shield up high.
And plant my feet unswervingly as the storm goes swirling by.
My hope is found in Jesus Christ who gives the victory!
I'll trust His goodness, power and love in this catastrophe.

I would not leave the path He's chosen, even if I could—
For I believe His promise—this will turn out for my good.
Time to stop the senseless squirming and surrender to His plan;
I'm silenced by His peace and joy as He holds me in His hand.

7/14/2008 N. Ferrin

One final thought about release – it doesn't happen just once. Years after the drive to Davenport, Mindy continued to struggle and squirm, resisting the love of the Savior and her family. She rejected the straight and narrow path, insisting on living on the edge. Surrender was a daily routine as I grew in understanding I was *not* responsible for her choices. For a long season, I never knew exactly where she was or how she was surviving. Her contact revolved around her need for money. While I attempted to hold firm boundaries and not enable, it was a heart-breaking choice each time she presented her case, seeking another rescue.

> Some time ago, Mindy decided to come home to live with me. She wanted a fresh start and I was relieved – *and scared*. Was she really ready for this needed change? Could I handle the impending changes to our home? Her dad brought her to my house while I was at an all-day class. As I drove home that day I anticipated the "welcome home hug" and it was sweet indeed. We moved her few things into the spacious third floor room and I thought, "This is so much better than what she's known for months. She'll be so happy to be here!" But that night the fear returned. Mindy left to spend time with friends and stayed out very late. One of my sons found me sobbing in my room, overcome with anxiety about my inadequacy to provide the support she needed. His words shattered my wall of fear and gave me refreshed

perspective. He said, "Don't allow her to control the climate of our home. Don't engage in her drama. Just go to sleep and let her come home whenever she chooses." I did, and I slept like a baby. *Release!*

The next day Mindy went to church with me but she was very restless and I sensed another fleeing. She wanted money and was very upset with me for not obliging. That afternoon she told me she was going to a movie, stuffed a change of clothes in her purse, and never returned. Her desire for "freedom" was too strong and she was gone.

Over and over again, I come face to face with this powerful truth – I cannot plan or control my prodigal's life. "Oh Lord, she is *Your* beloved child and You will protect and guide her. I know You are watching over Mindy with love." Release means giving up control and trusting in God's way and His timing. Not easy, but so necessary. Not once, but many times.

For Personal Reflection

1. As you pray for your prodigal, are you at the place of scheming, bargaining, pleading, or surrender?

2. How have you experienced God's peace in response to the release of your prodigal into His capable hands?

3. Are you more prone to be highly critical of your prodigal or do you race to the rescue? What might you try to change with God's help in these areas?

Pray: Instead of suggesting what God should do regarding your prodigal, spend time in prayer just resting in His presence and expressing your trust in His mighty hand.

Chapter Ten

Hope

Basic question: When will my prodigal come home?
Heart string: God can do all things; nothing is
impossible for Him.

There are many songs about hope. It is a recurring theme at most
churches and a favorite focus of retreats and seminars. I've spoken
on the topic many times. Tears have fallen as I've considered and
sung beautiful words like *"In Christ alone my hope is found. He is
my Light, my Strength, My song."* and *"My hope is built on nothing
less than Jesus' blood and righteousness . . . On Christ the solid Rock
I stand. All other ground is sinking sand."* These are such powerful,
foundational, sustaining truths. Yes, I have hope in Jesus! But do
I have hope related to my broken heart? Is there hope for those
who have strayed and for those who love them?

This chapter has been on hold for some time. I was not ready to
address the topic of hope because I was waiting for God's timing.
I thought I would write it after a great victory, when Mindy and
Danny were both on secure, upward paths, renewed in their faith
and desiring to live for Jesus. But that is not the Father's plan. *Now*

is the time is to write the final chapter, one that will not tie up all the loose ends into a beautiful bow. For faith is the substance of things *hoped* for, things we cannot yet see. There have been glimpses of hope, however. Many times the Lord pulls back the curtain and shows us He is at work. What joy floods the soul at those treasured times!

An otherwise routine car ride with Mindy took me by surprise and delighted my heart. She was living with a friend in another town and the new group of peers had been a healthy change. She spoke with a curious smile, "Guess what we were talking about last night? You'll never guess." "Give me a hint," I baited. "OK. It is something you'd like." I was afraid to say what I really hoped because the disappointment would sting. But she looked so happy and I wanted to see if it could be true. "The Lord?" I asked timidly. "YES!" She went on to give a few details about the conversation and then concluded, "I knew you'd be so proud of me for remembering so much from the bible." Proud of her??? Oh my, it went far beyond that. I was elated!! I was singing in my heart to the Lord, praising Him for His faithfulness. There *was* good seed planted in my precious daughter, and God was in charge of making it blossom. These sprouts, alone, were the most beautiful crop I'd seen in quite some time.

Evidence of God's power can easily be missed if we aren't paying attention. Recent bible studies have reminded me that God wants to communicate with us all the time. His voice can become familiar and frequent if we will take time to listen. In recent days I have been surprised by the wisdom and encouragement coming from my son, Danny. Slowly and steadily, almost without my notice, he is making much progress and is working hard to get his life back on track.

> There wasn't a sensational turning point for Danny. I vividly remember driving him awhile ago to the Vermont Teen Challenge with high hopes this would be the answer. After a very brief stay, he returned home and I was devastated. But now, looking back, he *did* begin to change significantly at that point in his life. One step at a time he is choosing a safer path. Today he is a young man with emotional strength and physical stamina. He works hard and loves sports. Along with one of his brothers, he adheres to a rigorous workout schedule, plays tennis, table tennis, and golf. He is also taking college courses in hopes of earning his degree. I'm so proud of him and I enjoy our math sessions as he perseveres through some preliminary courses.
>
> Also, within the past year he asked for a bible and I had one ready for him. I had purchased it not

knowing who it was for, but strongly convinced
by the Lord to buy it because He surely knew this
day was coming! In the following weeks, Danny
read the book of Daniel, along with some other
books by Dr. David Jeremiah as God continues
to plant good seed into his life. He has a deep
and genuine sensitivity and often knows when I
need a hug or a word of encouragement. While
he still has a "wild side", I cannot say that Danny
is a prodigal anymore. He has "returned home"
and I am so deeply thankful. I learned many
things during his rebellious years. One of the
most important lessons was that my plan is not
the only one or even the best one. God will fulfill
His promises for our children as we wait on Him
and place our hope in His unfailing love.

Joy and sorrow – laughter and pain, these are all a part of life.
The situation involving your prodigal may be only one part of
your current struggle. Sometimes the dips and detours of life
can lead to discouragement and despair. There are seasons when
hope can dim. When we don't see change on the horizon, it can
be difficult to maintain hope. Yet even in the darkest places, God
has surprising ways of reminding us He is at work and He will
not let us go.

After thirty years as a computer programmer,
my job ended when the system I supported

migrated to a newer platform. My job was no longer needed and I entered the ranks of the unemployed. Finding a new job was much harder than anticipated because I no longer had current, marketable programming skills. Financial pressures were mounting and on one particular day I was sinking fast. It was as if my balloon had been popped and hope was leaking out—quickly. Foreign, unwelcome, persistent thoughts entered my mind. "What good is all this Christianity anyways? Look where you are – no job; no spouse; no hope. Has it been worth all the years of bible study and teaching? Give it up!"

Suddenly the phone rang. I don't always answer when I'm in the midst of sadness, but this time I did. "Mom?" It was Mindy. "I saw your Facebook post and I just wanted to call and tell you that I want to help." How did she know from that post I was down in the dumps? She knows me better than I think. "Mom? Are you ok?" "Oh Mindy, you are so sweet. I'll be fine, but thank you for your concern." She proceeded to tell me about her long conversation the previous night with people who didn't know the Lord. My Mindy was defending the existence of God (again!)! She said I would have been so proud of her and she wished it had been taped for me to hear. She said,

"I told them there HAD to be a God because my mom has been teaching people about Him for years. She's been through tough stuff but she still believes in Him." The tears were racing down my cheeks but she couldn't see them on the other end of the phone. She didn't know how close I was to giving up. Her words infused pure hope into my soul. Suddenly all my struggles were minimized as I realized the significance of my reaction when hope was dim. *She is watching!* By God's grace and through His strength I *will not* let her down. "Dear Lord", I whispered after hanging up, "Thank You for not letting me get too far down into the pit of despair. Thank You for the reminder that others are watching. I want to stand firm in You. I trust You and I surrender once again to You. Thank You for the seeds that have been planted in the heart of my precious Mindy. She is Yours and my hope is in You."

As we all know, there are no guarantees in parenting. Seasons come and go, some bringing the sweetness of healing and others filled with the heartbreaking consequences of sinful choices. Pete Wilson's book, *Plan B*, has been a great source of hope in recent days. He discusses what we can do when God doesn't show up the way we thought He would. The goal is to find balance and hope in the midst of it all. Here are a few suggestions based on Wilson's book for embracing hope regardless of current circumstances:

- Remember that everyone has shattered dreams. We may think we are losing control when things don't work out the way we planned. But the truth is, we were never in control in the first place! Let's choose to acknowledge *God is in control* and He knows what He's doing.

- Renew your mind by seeking God's perspective. Wilson says, "We don't need the worry and anxiety that stresses us out and keeps us from really living. The trick is relearning what to fear and what not to fear, what's worth worrying about and what isn't." The way to find God's perspective in any situation is by spending time with Him in prayer and in His Word. It may also help to seek the counsel of godly friends.

- Rest in the truth that God is with you and that He can be trusted. We all have many questions as we journey through life and some will have no clear answers. Situations, people, opportunities will change, but through it all, God will never change. Wilson wisely says "our faith must rest on His identity and not necessarily His activity." There are two very different types of hope – one is hoping *for* something, the other is hoping *in* Someone. The first is bound to disappoint, the second will never fail.

Are you tempted to give up hope? Do you get tired, like me, when the wait gets longer and longer with little evidence of change? Do you sometimes feel alone in the struggle? Sharon Jaynes writes in her book, *Becoming a Woman Who Listens to God*, "On those days when I want to quit – I long for friends and family who will walk the course with me . . . But I know there will be many days that I will look around and discover there is no one there to cheer me on. That's when I need to look a bit closer, listen a bit more intently, and hear the still small voice of my heavenly Father. He's always there to pick me up when I fall, hold me when I cry, hug me when I'm feeling alone, cheer me when I'm victorious, and love me when I'm just me. Our heavenly Parent is cheering for you too, my friend. He's saying, 'Keep going! Don't give up! You are precious to Me! You're not alone! You can do it!'"

Oh friend, let's choose to persevere. We cannot possibly know what is ahead. Perhaps it is almost time for your new season of joy! Take a few more steps closer to Jesus. Press on in hope and find others for support and encouragement. Let the hope of Christ fill you because *He is with you* and *He is faithful.* My hope is in the One who loves my precious children even more than I, and He does His best work in seemingly hopeless situations. I can hardly wait to see what is ahead!

FOR PERSONAL REFLECTION

1. Are you a man or woman who listens to God? How do you know? What has He been saying to you recently?

2. What are some of the guarantees you once thought there were in parenting? How are your expectations changing?

3. How has God recently reminded you of His unchanging love for you? Begin to look for His "hugs" daily and give Him thanks for the big things and the small.

Pray: As you talk to the Father, rest in the assurance that He totally understands your situation in detail. Listen for His still small voice. Intercede for others who need you to cheer them on and ask the Lord how you can come alongside others to provide encouragement in the days ahead. Thank Him in advance for the ways He will redeem this painful season for His glory.

Final Reflections

Throughout their years on a prodigal path, both Mindy and Danny have been reminded of God's unconditional love and forgiveness available through Jesus Christ. They have also witnessed the strength and peace He has given their mother in good times and bad. Here are their thoughts about the journey and the importance of support, acceptance, and perseverance.

Looking back, what have you learned from the path you've walked?

Mindy: "I think the most important thing I have learned from the path I've chosen is the importance of the support system of my family. If not for all the help and tough love my family has shown me, my path could have been a lot rockier. I've learned my family will be there for me no matter what and I should never take that for granted. If there is one bridge you never want to burn it would be the one between you and your family."

Danny: "I have learned not to look back and dwell on my past. I have learned how to take the good from it and how to continue forging a new path in the right direction."

Have you seen evidence of God's love and protection on your journey?
If so, how/where/when?

Mindy: "Looking back at everything I have been through, I think the only thing that kept me safe, out of jail, and alive was God's love. There have been a lot of points in my past where I have seen His protection. He has never failed me and every time I have prayed for help it has been given. Often the help didn't come the way I wanted, but the tough lessons are the ones that help you learn in the long run. I would say I am extremely lucky and grateful to be able to say I trust in God and I have seen His unconditional love in many different ways throughout my rebellion."

Danny: "There have been beacons of light along my journey. Sometimes I would choose to ignore it, and other times ignoring it wasn't possible. There were many nights either in my car, a hospital, or even at my mother's house where waking up the next morning did not seem like a guarantee. I remember praying to be given another chance, if I could just survive the night. There were also many nights where my ride home could have ended in disaster. While not every situation involved life and death, they are the ones that stick out in your mind when you reflect on how far you've come. It's amazing what I missed and ignored while finding my way."

What message would you give to parents of prodigals?

Mindy: "There are some words of advice I would give parents of prodigals. No matter how hard it is sometimes, tough love is the only way to get through to your kid. They may not see it at the time, but trust me, I now wish I had listened and obeyed everything my mother told me when I was beginning my journey as a prodigal. Also, along with tough love, be as close and understanding as possible. You may be worried and cautious, but what really helped me was the friendship between me and my mom. I always know she will be there to talk to me and try to understand where I am coming from. She won't always agree, but the fact that she listens and shares her thoughts and opinions helps me think through tough situations. It is very important in my eyes to keep that bond."

Danny: "I'm sure you've heard it before, but don't blame yourself for not being able to 'snap them out of it'. The one thing that stuck out to me about my mother along the way was her forgiveness and her commitment to do anything in her power to help me. I took advantage of her and hurt her. Despite the things I did, she never failed in her approach. I admire that most. She was always my biggest fan and she never gave up on me."

Is there anything else you would like to share?

Mindy: "As a prodigal, I have not yet fully returned to safety and my unconditionally loving mother. I am still going through the daily battles, but I have also calmed down considerably and better days are ahead. So parents, it doesn't last forever. Even though you are going through some hard times, it will end. Your kids will realize and appreciate the love you have for them and God's love for them. Don't lose hope. Keep trusting that God will have an impact and change their lives."

Danny: "I didn't choose the easiest path through life, and I am still paying for the mistakes I have made. Even given the setbacks, I couldn't be happier where I am in life. I have a renewed sense of purpose and direction. If I slip, I know that God, and my mother, will be right there to pick me back up."

Mindy and Danny, Sept 2012

CLOSING BLESSING

Dear Loving, Heavenly Father,

I pray for those who have read this book and who are in need of encouragement and hope. Please, Lord, give them a renewed perspective. Help them to trust in your goodness, faithfulness, patience and love. Guide them day by day to do the next thing. Provide ongoing strength and insight for each situation. Free them from the burden of guilt and shame. Give them rest in your strong, protective arms and hope for a new day coming.

I also pray for our beloved prodigals, Lord. You know them all by name and your love for them far exceeds ours. Watch over them. Protect them from the enemy. Lift them up from the pit and place their feet upon a firm path. Show them how precious they are. Give them reassurance that they are always welcome home!! May they feel your peace and find your sustaining grace. Bless them and show them the way.

For all these things we give our thanks. We choose this day to trust You for all that is ahead. Thank You for the promises and hope we have in You.

In the powerful, redeeming Name of Jesus, Amen!

Contact Information:

Please let me know how I can be praying for your situation. Contact me via email at nancy.ferrin@comcast.net or visit my website: steppingcloser.com. I also have a blog, "Encouragement for the Journey" at this link: http://nancyferrin.wordpress.com/

Blessings to you!!

RECOMMENDED RESOURCES

Dobson, Dr. James, *When God Doesn't Make Sense.* Tyndale House, 1997.

Dillow, Linda, *Calm My Anxious Heart.* NAV Press, 2007.

Gregston, Mark, *When Your Teen is Struggling.* Harvest House Publishers, 2007.

Jaynes, Sharon, *Becoming A Woman Who Listens to God.* Harvest House Publishers, 2012.

Jeremiah, Dr. David, *Slaying the Giants in Your Life.* Thomas Nelson Publishers, 2008.

Kraft, Vickie, *Facing Your Feelings.* Thomas Nelson Publishers, 1996.

MacDonald, James, *Turning Your Trials to Gold.* Walk in the Word, 2009.

Ortberg, John, *When the Game is Over, It All Goes Back in the Box.* Zondervan, 2007.

Partow, Donna, *Becoming a Vessel God Can Use.* Bethany House Publishers, 2004.

Waldrep, Phil, *Parenting Prodigals.* Baxter Press, 2001.

Wilson, Pete, *Plan B . . . What Do You Do When God Doesn't Show Up the Way You Thought He Would?* Thomas Nelson Publishers, 2010.